SCHOLASTIC
Learning Express

Shapes and Patterns

This book belongs to

_____

First edition 2012
Reprinted 2012

ISBN 978-981-07-1352-2

Welcome to Learning Express!

Helping your child build essential skills is easy!

These teacher-approved activities have been specially developed to make learning both accessible and enjoyable. On each page, you'll find:

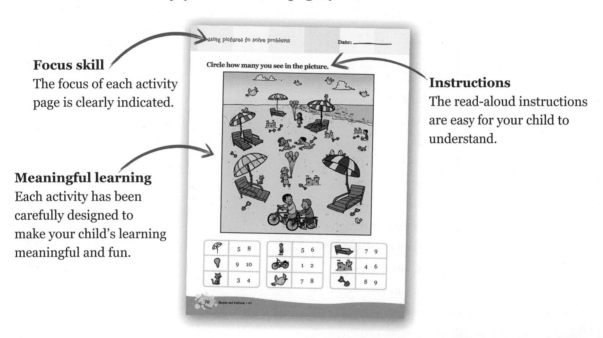

Focus skill
The focus of each activity page is clearly indicated.

Instructions
The read-aloud instructions are easy for your child to understand.

Meaningful learning
Each activity has been carefully designed to make your child's learning meaningful and fun.

This book also contains:

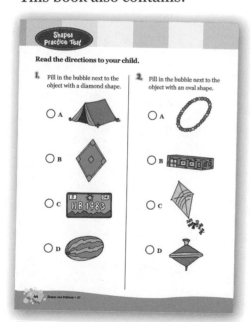

Completion certificate to celebrate your child's leap in learning.

Instant assessment to ensure your child really masters the skills.

Motivational stickers to mark the milestones of your child's learning path.

Contents

Shapes

Recognizing shapes is the basic foundation of geometry skills. Being able to draw shapes helps children develop fine motor skills and also learn the basic strokes used in letter formation.

What to Do
Read the directions on each page to your child. When he or she is finished, help your child check his or her work. Offer lots of praise for being such a "super shape kid!"

Keep On Going!
• Challenge your child to find certain shapes around them; for instance, wheels, clocks and lights on a stop light are all circles.
• Cut colored paper into different shapes and have your child paste them onto a larger sheet of paper to make a shape collage.

Date: _____

Trace and color the circles.

Date: _____

Find the circles. Color them red.

Date: _____

Trace the balls. Draw four more balls.

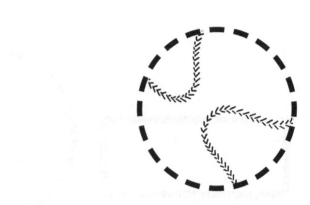

Date: _____

Trace and color the squares.

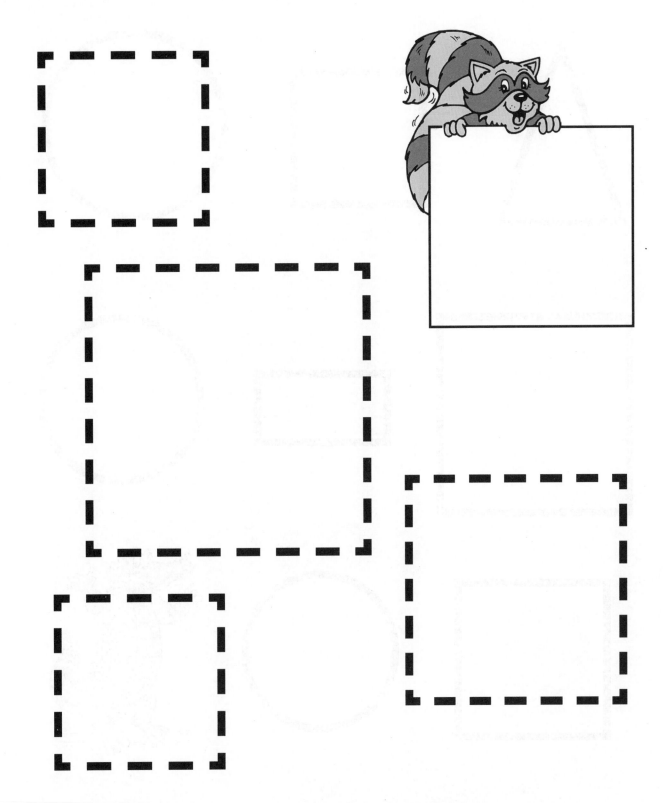

Date: _____

Find the squares. Color them blue.

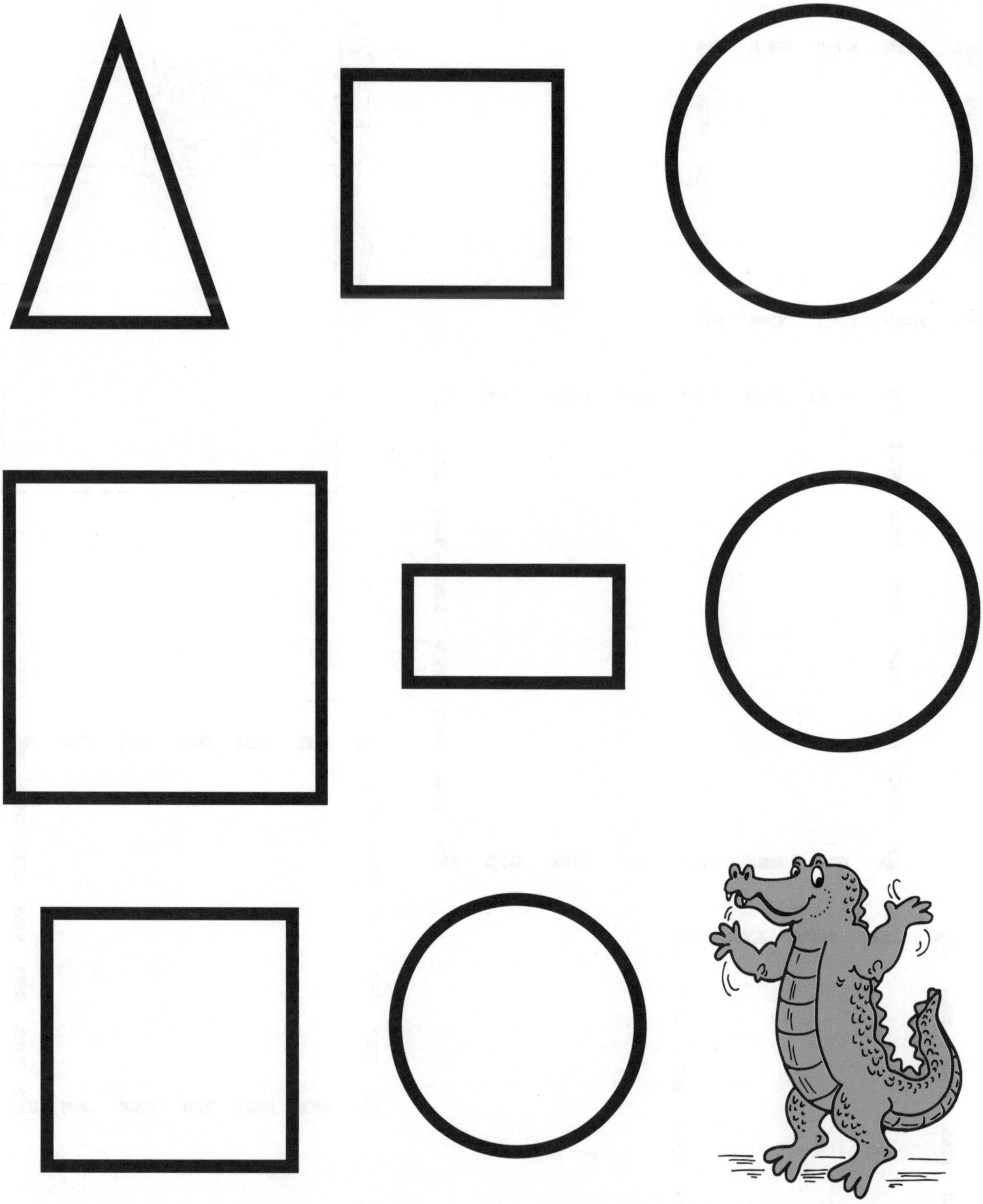

Date: _____

Trace and color the squares.

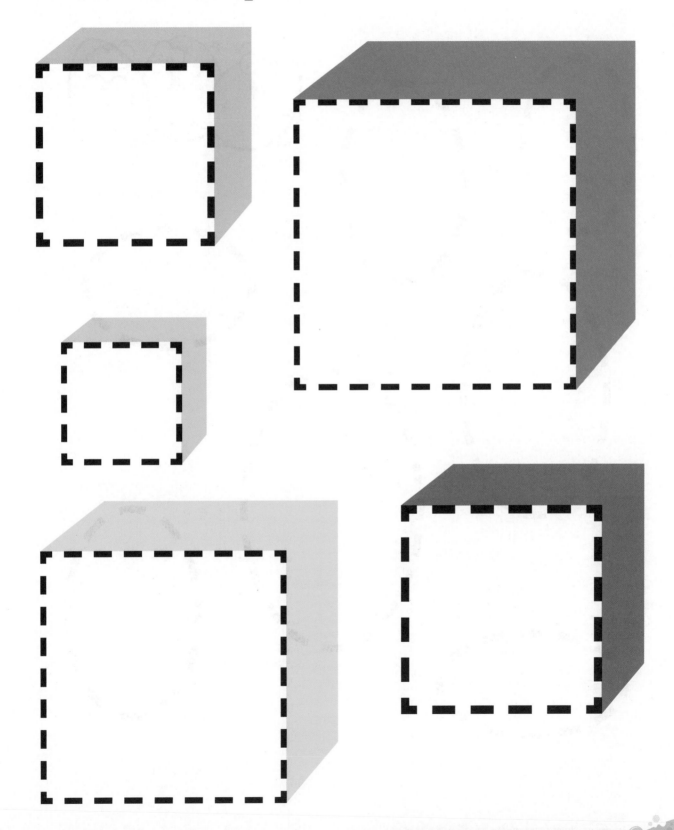

Date: _____

Trace and color the ovals.

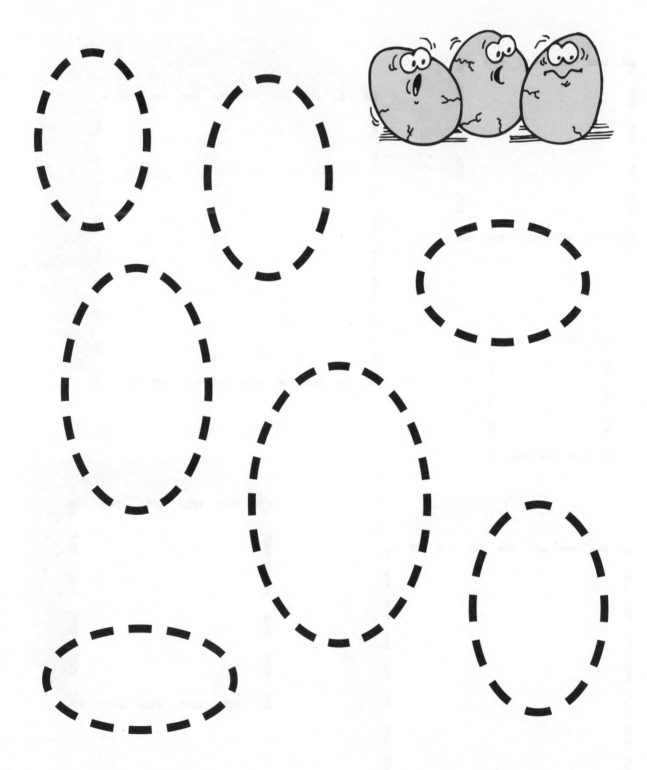

Date: _____

Find the ovals. Color them yellow.

Draw five oval eggs. Color each egg.

Date: _____

Trace and color the rectangles.

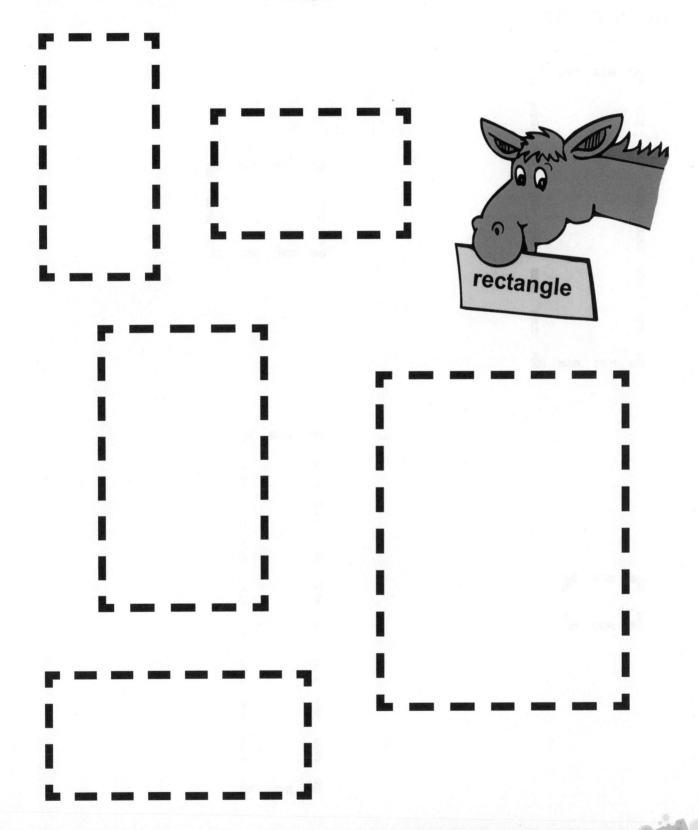

rectangle

Date: _____

Trace each rectangle. Draw a rectangle in each box just like the first one.

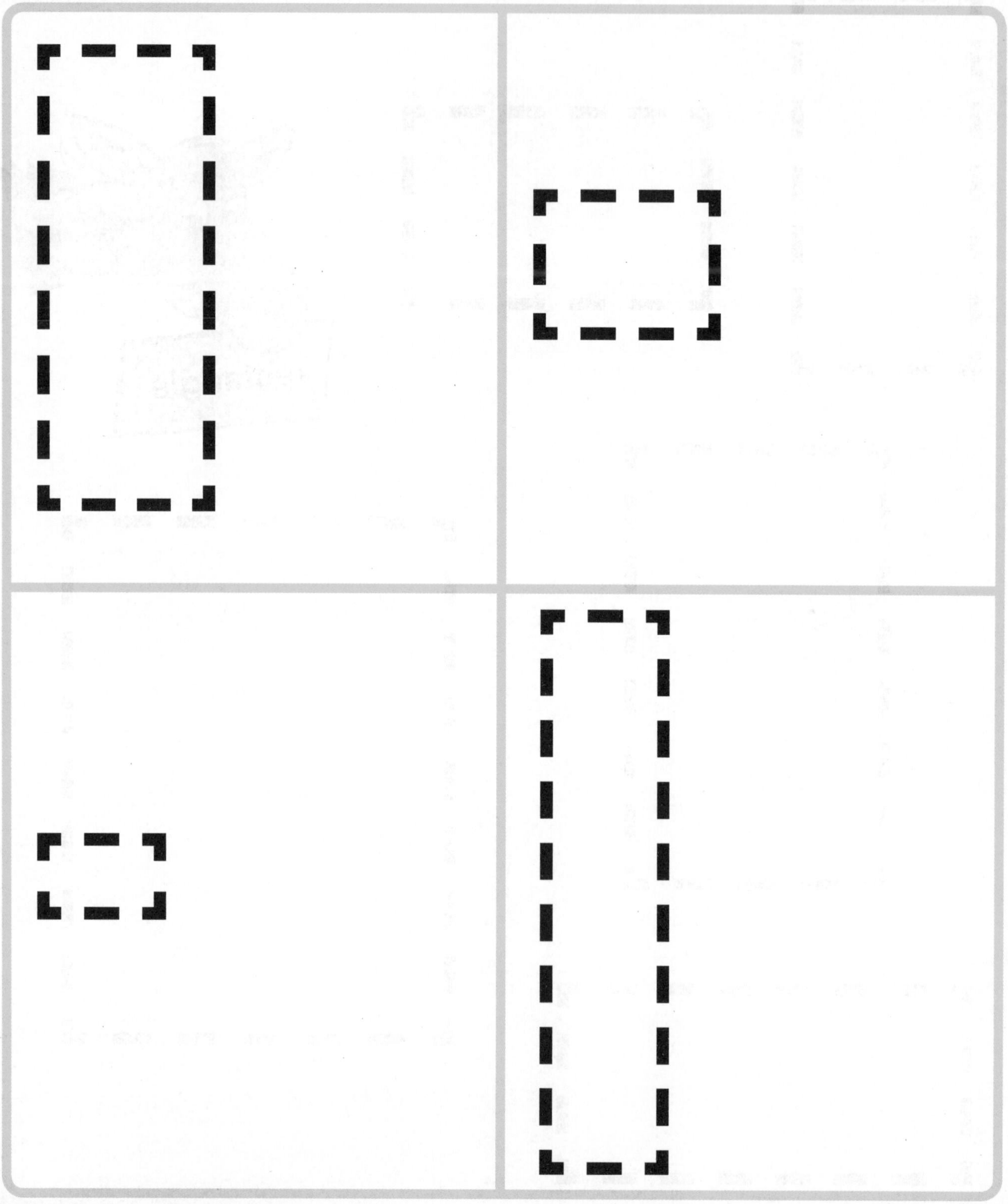

Date: _____

Find the rectangles. Color them red.

Date: _____

Trace and color the triangles.

Date: _____

Trace the wings of each butterfly.

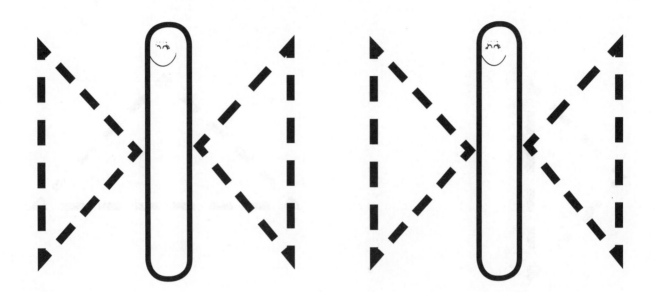

Draw wings for the butterflies. Color the butterflies.

Date: _____

Trace each triangle. Draw a triangle in each box just like the first one.

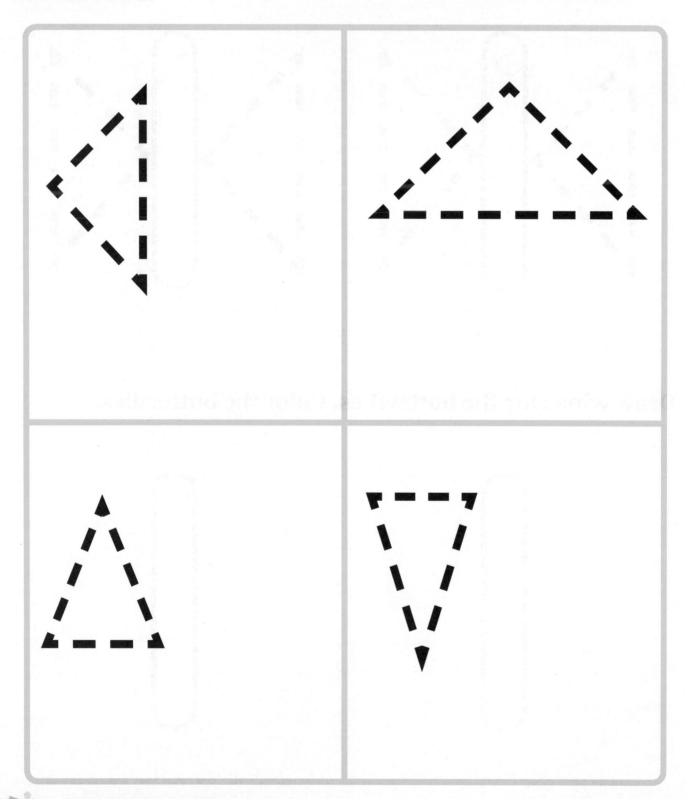

Trace and color the diamonds.

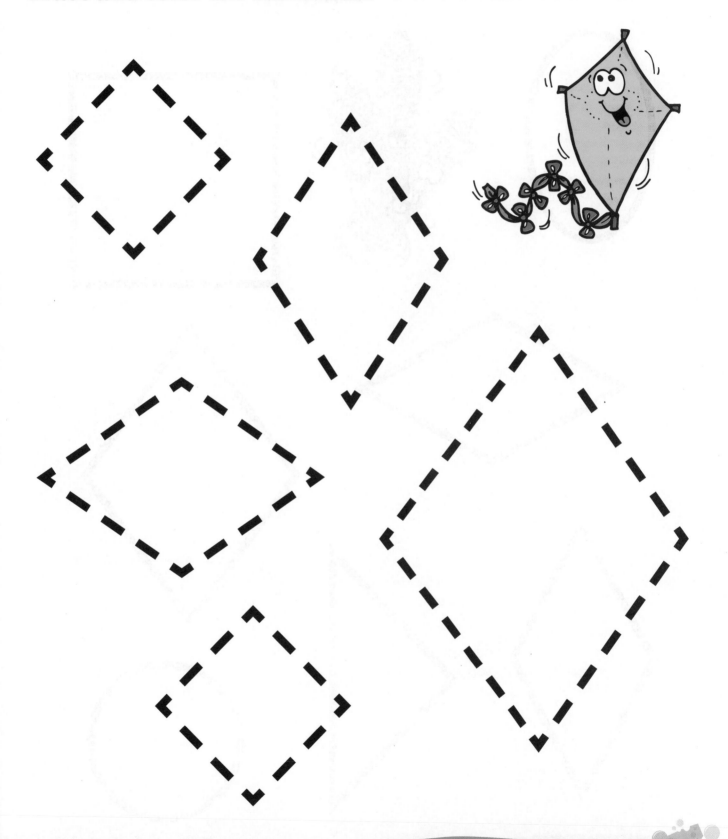

Find the diamonds. Color them green.

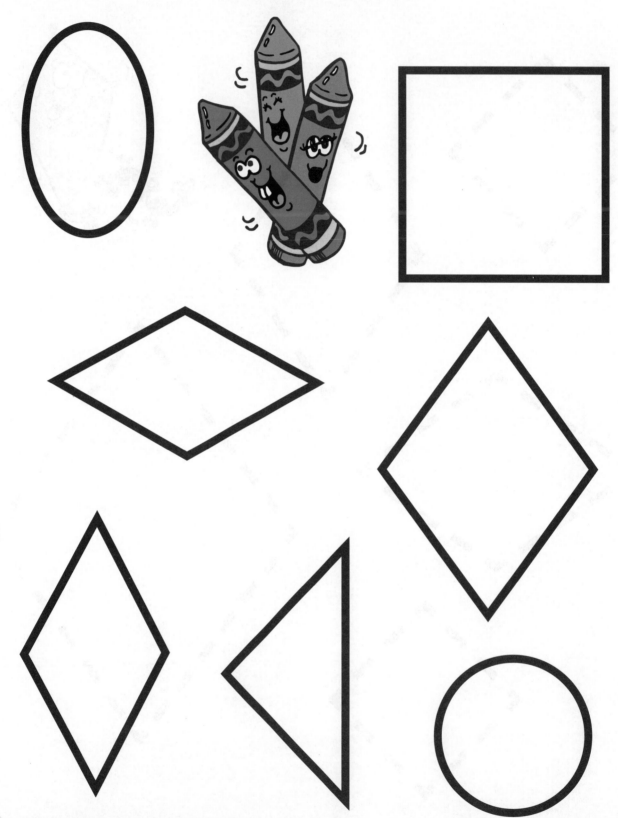

Trace and color each kite.

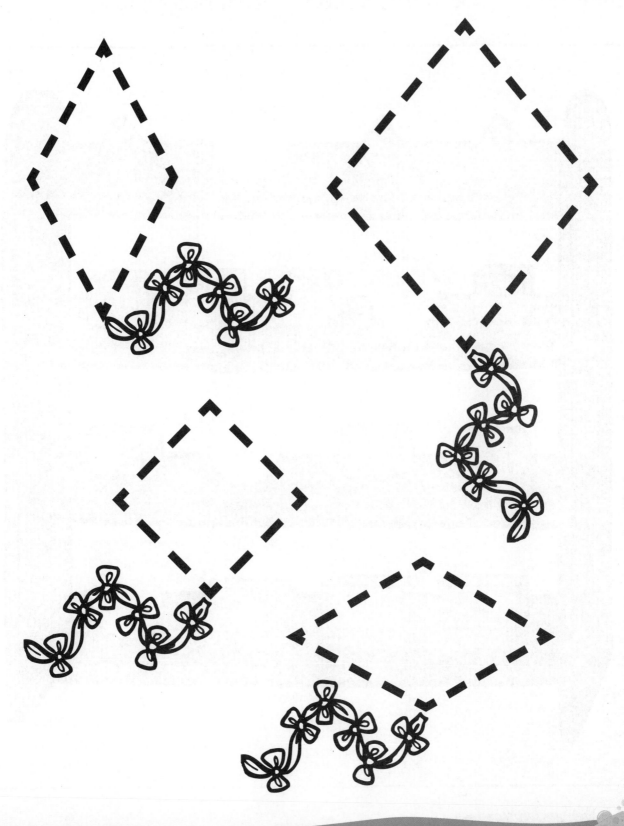

Date: _____

It's time to put away the blocks.
Paste each block on the shelf where it belongs.

Date: _____

How many of each shape are there in the snowflake?

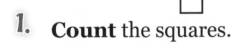

1. **Count** the squares.

2. **Write** the number. _____

3. **Count** the triangles.

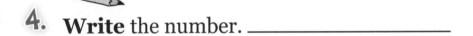

4. **Write** the number. _____

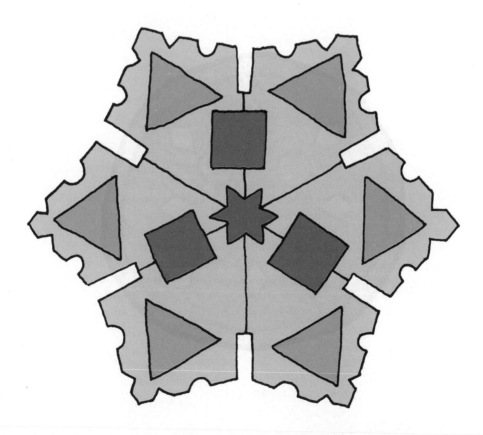

Date: _____

How many of each shape are there in the pizza?

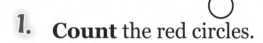

1. **Count** the red circles.

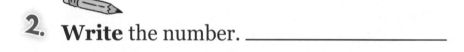

2. **Write** the number. _____

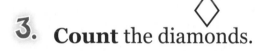

3. **Count** the diamonds.

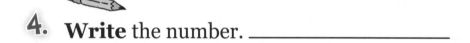

4. **Write** the number. _____

Date: _____

How many of each shape are there in the robot?

1. **Count** the rectangles.

2. **Write** the number. _____

3. **Count** the ovals.

4. **Write** the number. _____

Date: _____

Trace and color all the shapes. Say each shape's name.

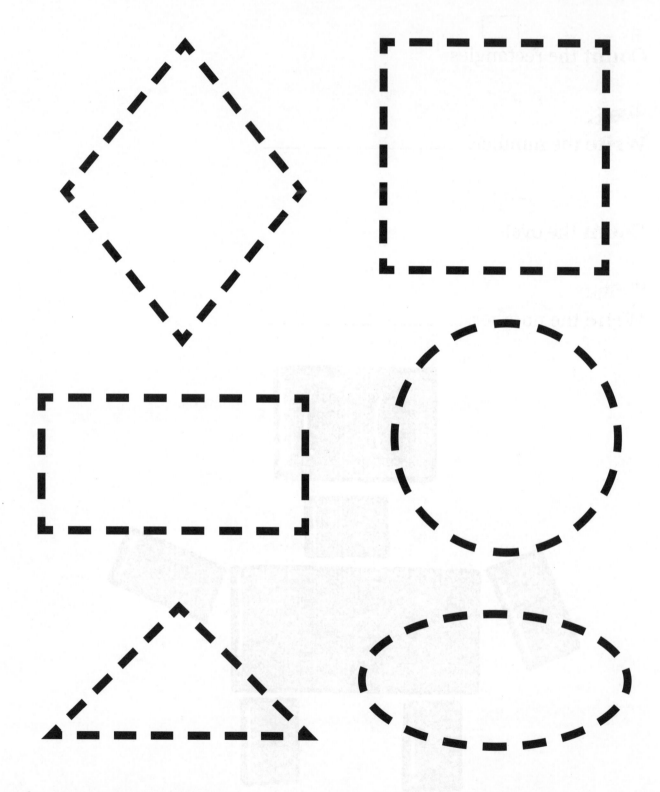

Put an X on each object with a circle shape.

Date: _____

Circle each object with a square shape.

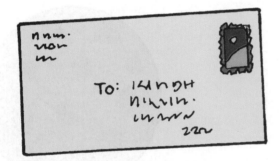

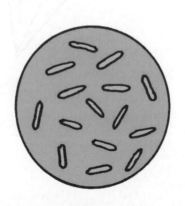

Date: _____

Circle each object with a rectangle shape.

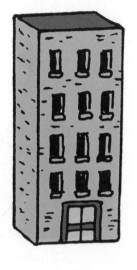

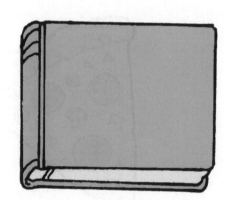

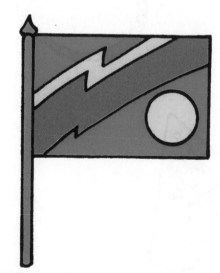

Date: _____

Circle each object with a triangle shape.

Date: _____

Circle each object with a diamond shape.

Date: _____

Circle each object with an oval shape.

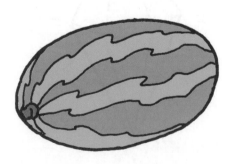

Date: _____

Trace each shape. Draw a line to match each object to its shape. Color the objects.

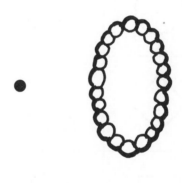

Date: _____

Color each circle ◯ to show the mole's way home.

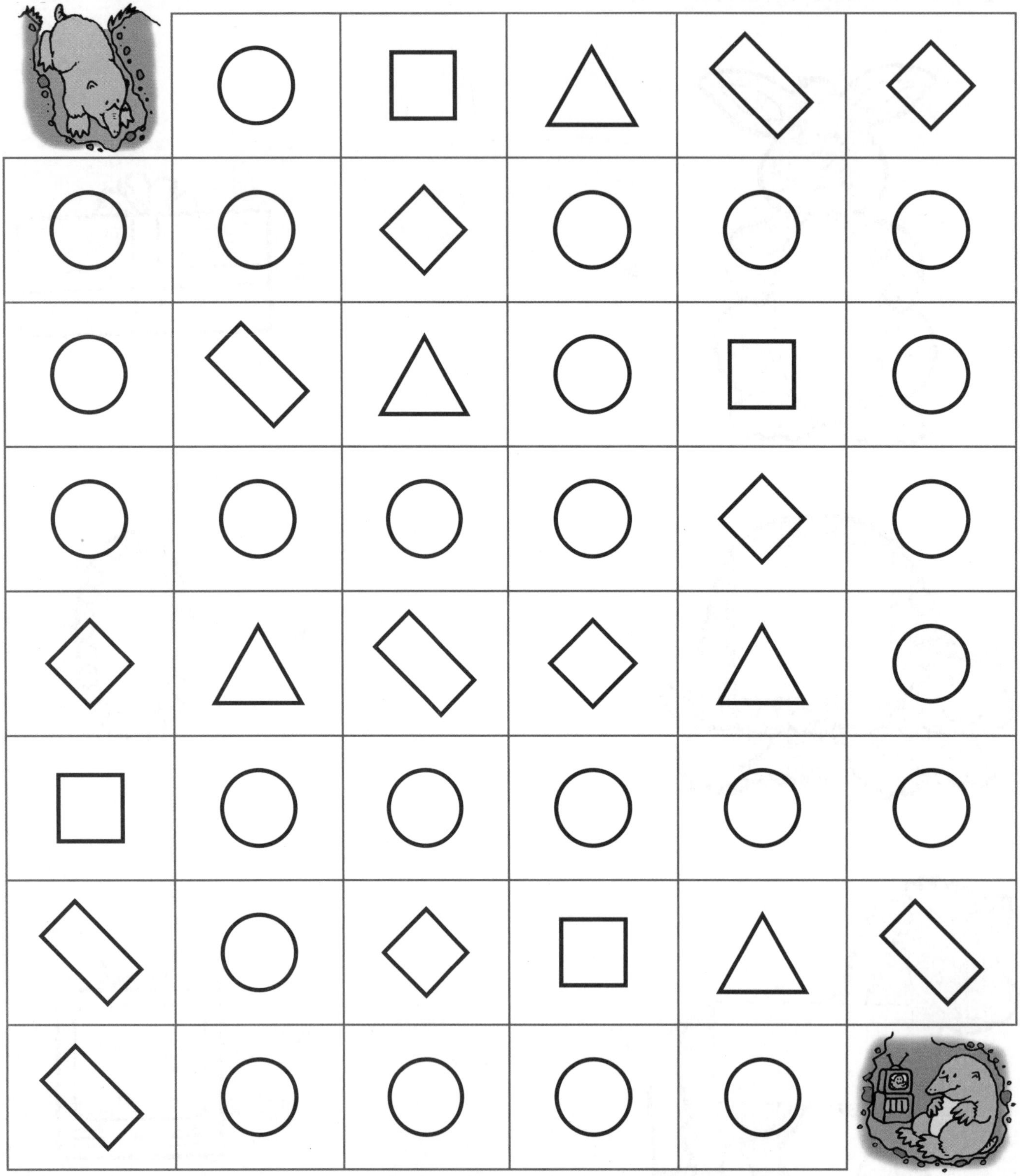

Date: —————————

Color each square ☐ to show the bee's way to the honeycomb.

Date: _____

Color each oval ◯ to show the frog's way to the lily pad.

Date: _____

Color each rectangle ▢ to show the cricket's way home.

Date: _____

Color each triangle △ green to show what the hidden picture is.

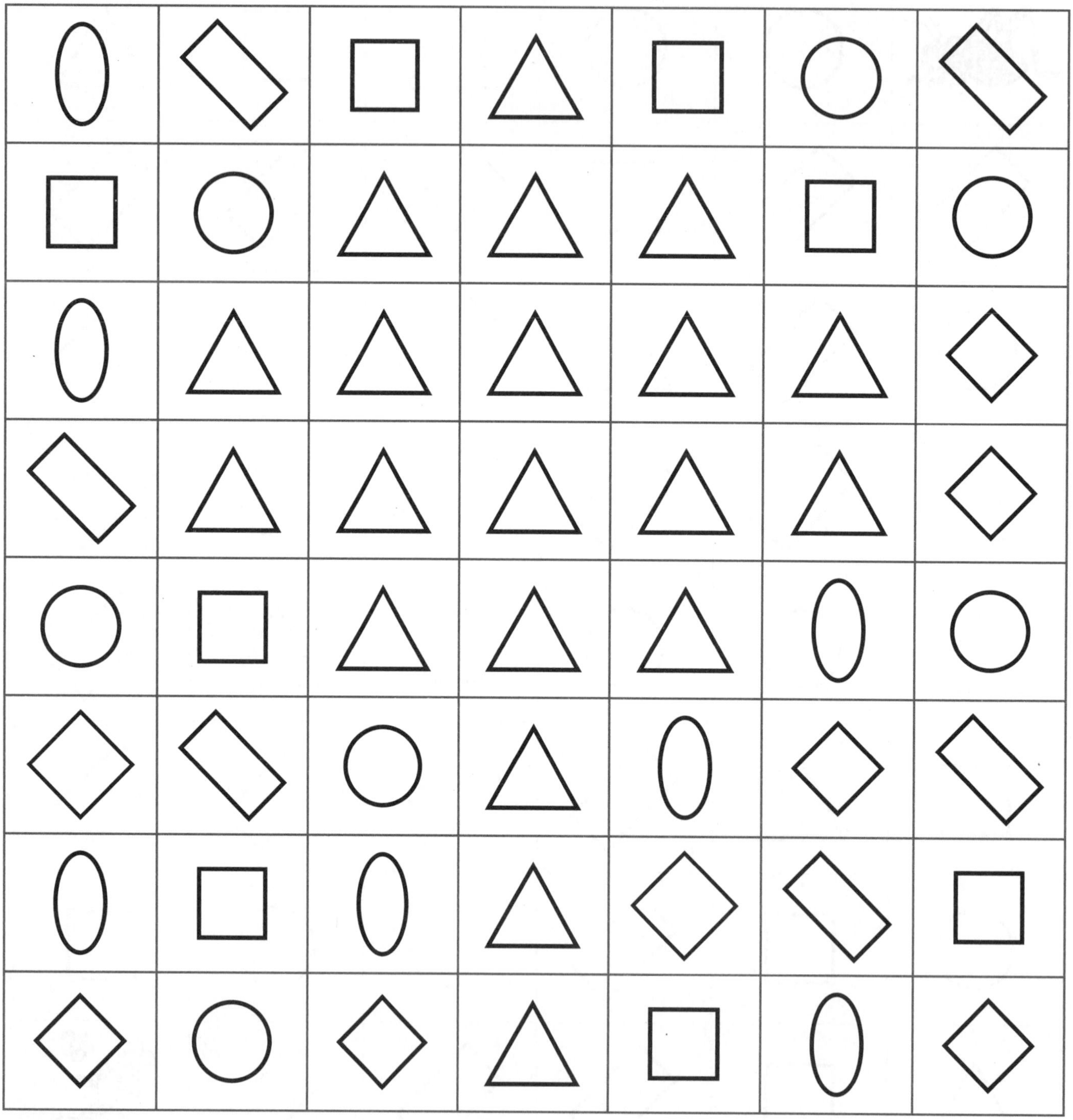

⬭	◇	☐	△	☐	◯	◇
☐	◯	△	△	△	☐	◯
⬭	△	△	△	△	△	◇
◇	△	△	△	△	△	◇
◯	☐	△	△	△	⬭	◯
◇	◇	◯	△	⬭	◇	◇
⬭	☐	⬭	△	◇	◇	☐
◇	◯	◇	△	☐	⬭	◇

 What is the hidden picture?

Date: _____

Color each diamond ◇ yellow to show what the hidden letter is.

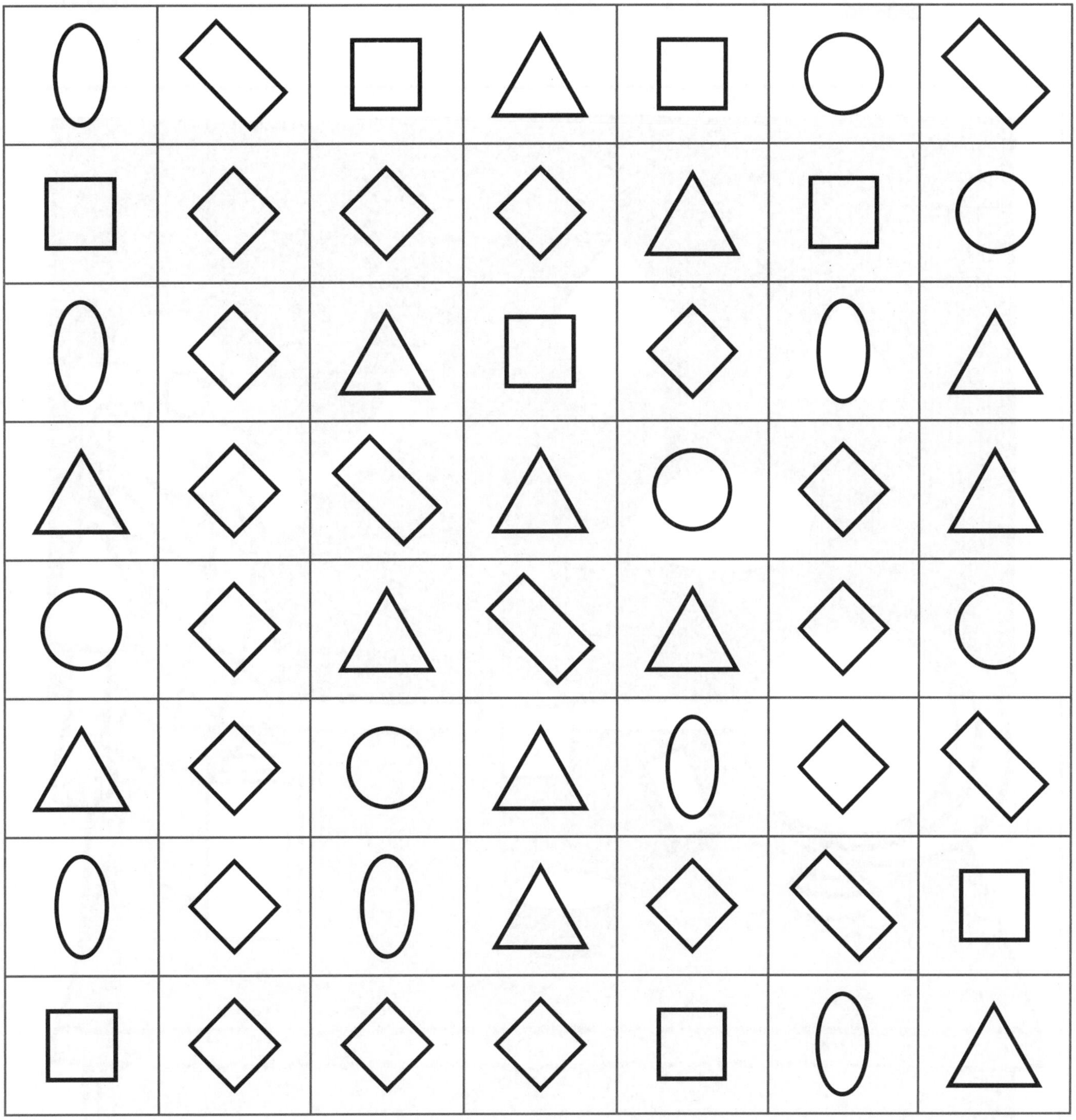

What is the hidden letter?

Date: _____

Color. = black ◼ = blue ▲ = red

◼ = brown ● = green ⬭ = yellow

Color. 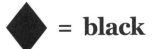 = black   ■ = blue   ▲ = red

      ▬ = brown   ● = green   ⬭ = yellow

Read the directions to your child.

1. Fill in the bubble next to the object with a diamond shape.

○ A

○ B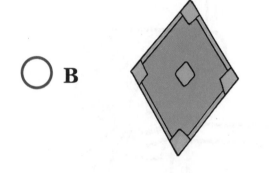

○ C

○ D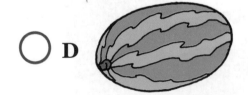

2. Fill in the bubble next to the object with an oval shape.

○ A

○ B

○ C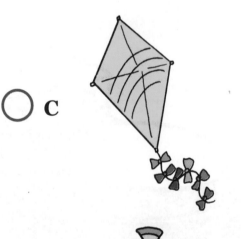

○ D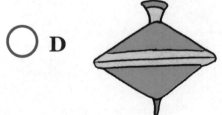

Shapes Practice Test

Read the directions to your child.

3. Fill in the bubble next to the object with a rectangle shape.

○ A

○ B

○ C

○ D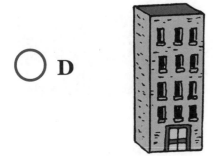

4. Fill in the bubble next to the object with a triangle shape.

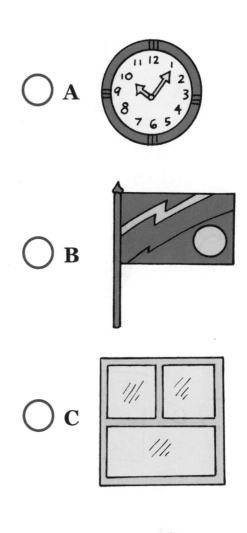

○ A

○ B

○ C

○ D

Read the directions to your child.

5. Fill in the bubble next to the object with a circle shape.

○ A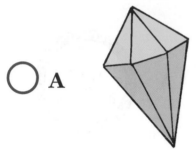

○ B

○ C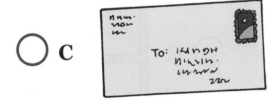

○ D

6. Fill in the bubble next to the object with a square shape.

○ A

○ B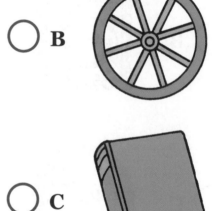

○ C

○ D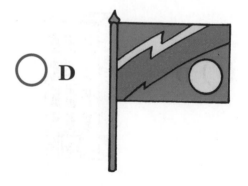

Read the directions to your child.

7. Count the number of circles. Fill in the bubble next to the correct number.

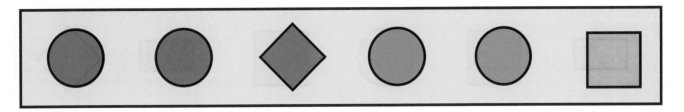

○ **A** 1   ○ **C** 3

○ **B** 2   ○ **D** 4

8. Count the number of triangles. Fill in the bubble next to the correct number.

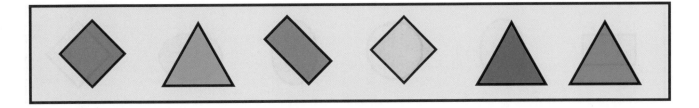

○ **A** 1   ○ **C** 3

○ **B** 2   ○ **D** 4

Read the directions to your child.

9. Count the number of squares. Fill in the bubble next to the correct number.

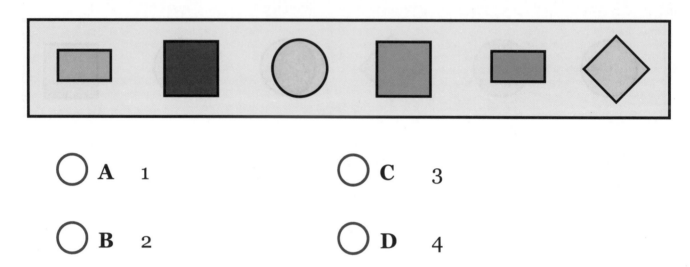

○ **A**   1   ○ **C**   3

○ **B**   2   ○ **D**   4

10. Count the number of ovals. Fill in the bubble next to the correct number.

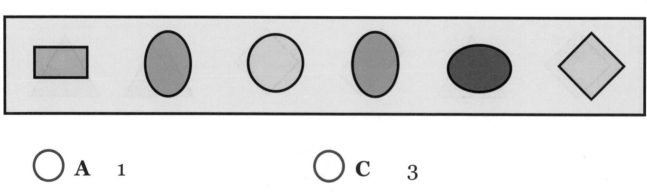

○ **A**   1   ○ **C**   3

○ **B**   2   ○ **D**   4

Read the directions to your child.

11. Count the number of rectangles. Fill in the bubble next to the correct number.

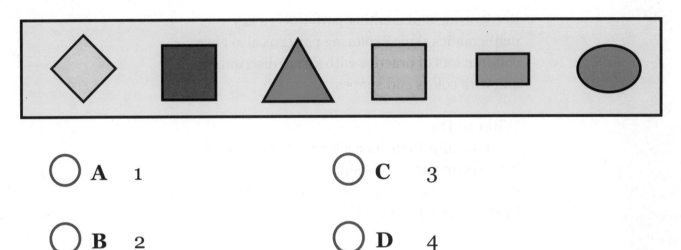

   ○ **A**   1   ○ **C**   3

   ○ **B**   2   ○ **D**   4

12. Count the number of diamonds. Fill in the bubble next to the correct number.

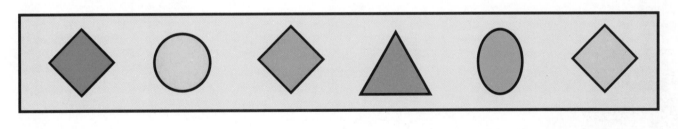

   ○ **A**   1   ○ **C**   3

   ○ **B**   2   ○ **D**   4

Patterns

Recognizing and creating patterns is a key mathematics skill. Exploring patterns also gives children lots of practice with visual discrimination and with colors and shapes.

What to Do

Read the directions on each page to your child. When he or she is finished, help your child check his or her work. Offer lots of praise for being such a "good pattern detective!"

Keep On Going!

Invite your child to find patterns in the world around them: stripes on a zebra, plaid patterns on clothing and so on.

Date: _____

Draw a line to the shape that comes next.

1.

2.

3.

4.

5.

Date: _____

Circle what comes next.

1.

2.

3.

4.

5.

Date: _____

Circle what comes next.

1.

2.

3.

4.

5.

Date: _____

Circle what comes next.

1. |

2. |

3. |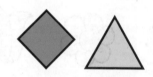

4. |

5. |

identifying patterns

Date: _____

Draw what comes next in the box at the end of each row.

Example

1.

2.

3.

Date: _____

Draw what comes next in the box at the end of each row.

1.

2.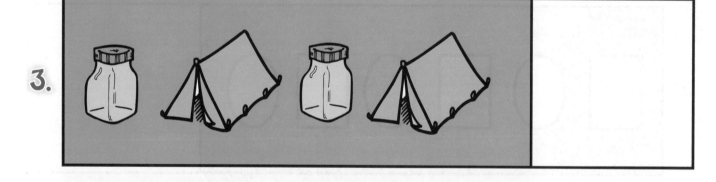

3.

4.

Read the directions to your child.

1. What comes next in the pattern? Fill in the bubble to show your answer.

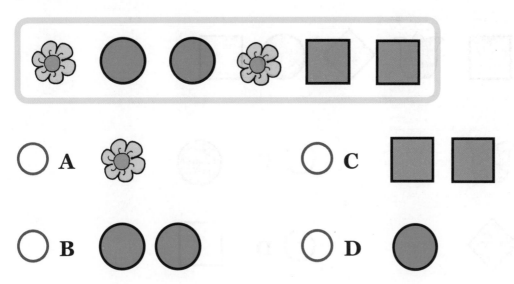

2. What comes next in the pattern? Fill in the bubble to show your answer.

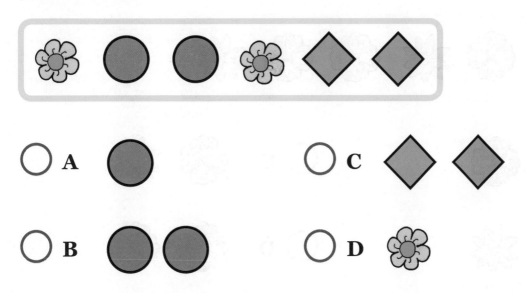

Read the directions to your child.

3. What comes next in the pattern? Fill in the bubble to show your answer.

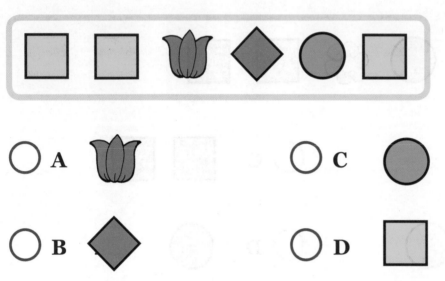

○ A

○ B

○ C

○ D

4. What comes next in the pattern? Fill in the bubble to show your answer.

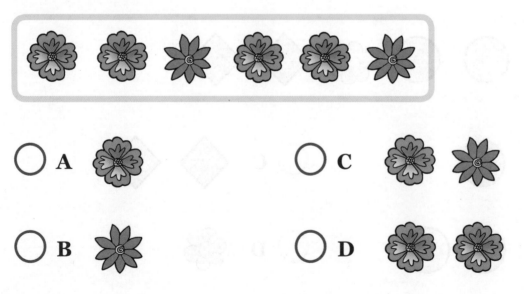

○ A

○ B

○ C

○ D

Read the directions to your child.

5. What comes next in the pattern? Fill in the bubble to show your answer.

⟡ **A**

⟡ **C**

⟡ **B**

⟡ **D**

6. What comes next in the pattern? Fill in the bubble to show your answer.

⟡ **A**

⟡ **C**

⟡ **B**

⟡ **D**

Read the directions to your child.

7. What comes next in the pattern? Fill in the bubble to show your answer.

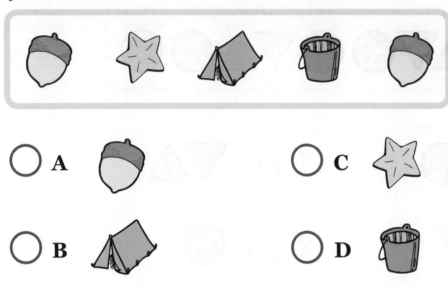

○ A

○ B

○ C

○ D

8. What comes next in the pattern? Fill in the bubble to show your answer.

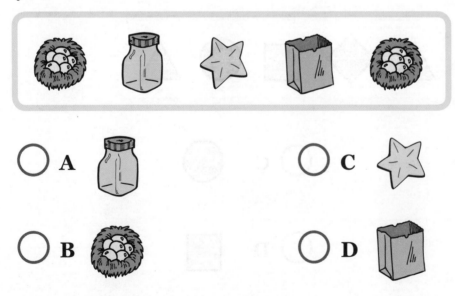

○ A

○ B

○ C

○ D

Problem Solving

Problem solving is a key skill that children can apply in all school subjects and in their daily lives. In this section, children use pictures to solve problems.

What to Do
Read the directions on each page to your child. When he or she is finished, help your child check his or her work. Offer lots of praise for being such a "good problem solver!"

Keep On Going!
• Put together various puzzles with your child.
• Point out certain instances in which pictures can help your child understand the meaning of words they can't read yet. For instance, point out street signs with symbols that mean "Don't Walk."

Paste the stickers in the correct places to make a hot dog like the one in the picture below.

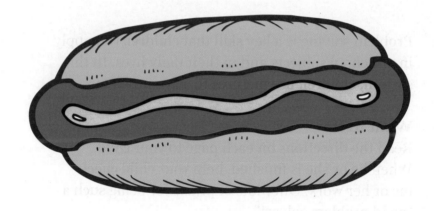

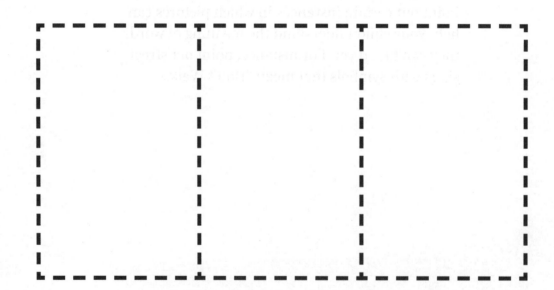

Date: _____

Paste the stickers in the correct places to make a pencil like the one in the picture below.

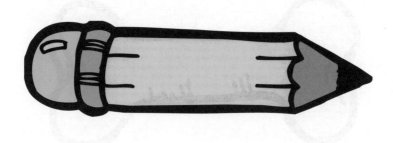

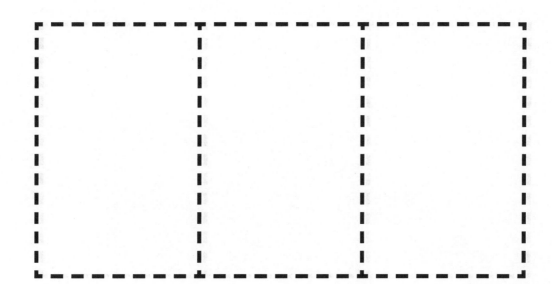

Date: _____

Paste the stickers in the correct places to make a bone like the one in the picture below.

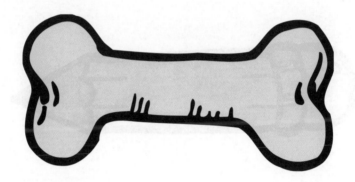

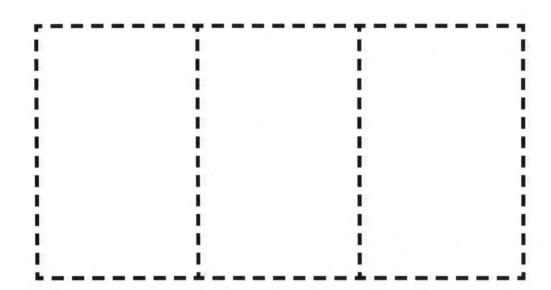

Date: _____

Paste the stickers in the correct places to make a watermelon like the one in the picture below.

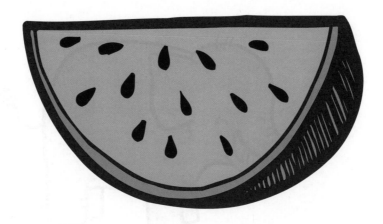

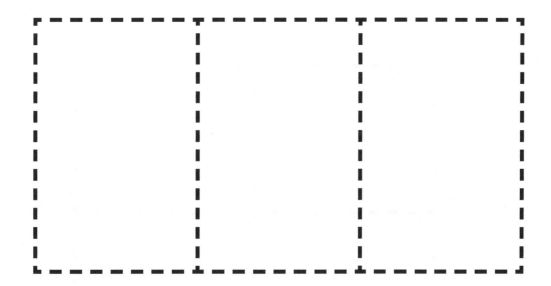

Date: _____

Paste the stickers in the correct places to make an elephant like the one in the picture below.

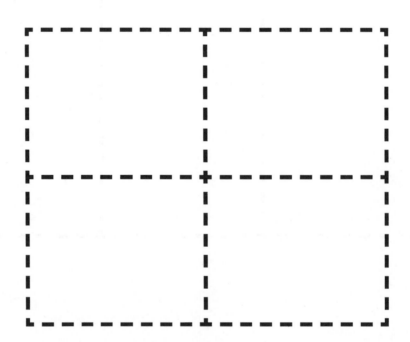

Date: _____

Paste the stickers in the correct places to make a house like the one in the picture below.

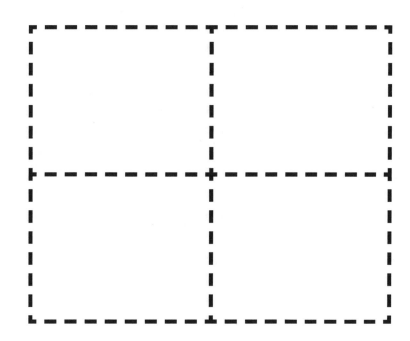

Date: _____

Paste the stickers in the correct places to make a vase like the one in the picture below.

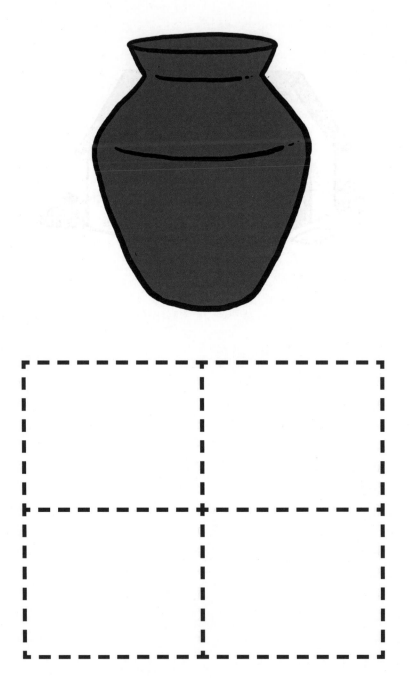

Date: _____

Paste the stickers in the correct places to make a clown's face like the one in the picture below.

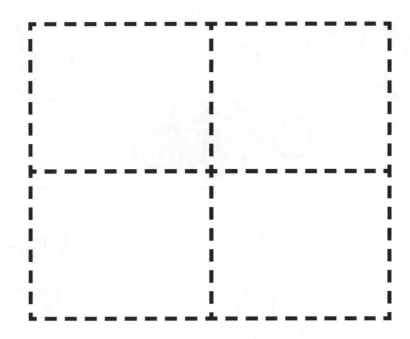

Date: _____

Circle how many you see in the picture.

🏖️	5	8
🎈	9	10
🐱	3	4

🧍	5	6
🚲	1	2
🐦	7	8

🛋️	7	9
🏰	4	6
🪏	8	9

Date: _____

Look at the picture.

How many do you see?
Write the number.

Date: _____

Look at the picture.

How many do you see?
Write the number.

Read the directions to your child.

1. Fill in the bubble next to the number of circles in the picture.

    ○ **A** 6

    ○ **B** 7

    ○ **C** 8

    ○ **D** 9

2. Fill in the bubble next to the number of diamonds in the picture.

    ○ **A** 6

    ○ **B** 7

    ○ **C** 8

    ○ **D** 9

Read the directions to your child.

3. Fill in the bubble next to the number of ovals at the bottom of the picture.

◯ **A**   6

◯ **B**   7

◯ **C**   8

◯ **D**   9

5. Fill in the bubble next to the number of blue squares between the two towers.

◯ **A**   2

◯ **B**   3

◯ **C**   4

◯ **D**   5

4. Fill in the bubble next to the number of triangles around the sun.

◯ **A**   7

◯ **B**   8

◯ **C**   9

◯ **D**   10

6. Fill in the bubble next to the number of circles in the castle.

◯ **A**   1

◯ **B**   2

◯ **C**   3

◯ **D**   4

Read the directions to your child.

7. Fill in the bubble next to the number of squares in the picture.

○ **A** 1

○ **B** 2

○ **C** 3

○ **D** 4

8. Fill in the bubble next to the number of triangles in the picture.

○ **A** 4

○ **B** 5

○ **C** 6

○ **D** 7

Read the directions to your child.

9. Fill in the bubble next to the number of rectangles in the picture.

    ◯ **A**   7

    ◯ **B**   8

    ◯ **C**   9

    ◯ **D**   10

11. Fill in the bubble next to the number of circles in the picture.

    ◯ **A**   7

    ◯ **B**   8

    ◯ **C**   9

    ◯ **D**   10

10. Fill in the bubble next to the number of ovals in the picture.

    ◯ **A**   3

    ◯ **B**   4

    ◯ **C**   5

    ◯ **D**   6

12. Fill in the bubble next to the number of diamonds in the picture.

    ◯ **A**   4

    ◯ **B**   5

    ◯ **C**   6

    ◯ **D**   7

Answer Key

Shapes

Page 6-23

Review that all shapes are traced, colored and drawn according to the directions.

Page 24

Review that shapes are pasted onto appropriate shelves.

Page 25

2. 3   4. 6

Page 26

2. 4   4. 8

Page 27

2. 7   4. 2

Page 28-43

Review that directions have been followed.

Page 44-49

1. B	2. A	3. D	4. D
5. B	6. A	7. D	8. C
9. B	10. C	11. A	12. C

Patterns

Page 51

1. circle   2. oval

3. square   4. rectangle

5. triangle

Page 52

1. shirt   2. belt

3. skirt   4. shoes

5. hat

Page 53

1. pink flower   2. green flower

3. orange flower   4. yellow flower

5. yellow flower

Page 54

1. square   2. rectangle

3. triangle   4. square

5. circle

Page 55

1. square

2. rectangle

3. hexagon

Page 56

1. acorn   2. star

3. jar   4. pail

Page 57-60

1. A	2. D	3. D	4. D
5. B	6. B	7. C	8. A

Problem Solving

Page 62-69

Review that pictures are pasted in the correct order.

Page 70

5 umbrellas, 10 balloons, 3 cats

5 boys, 2 bicycles, 8 birds

7 deckchairs, 4 sandcastles, 9 shovels

Page 71

6 snails, 3 goldfish, 5 sea urchins

4 guppies, 1 clump of seaweed, 6 pebbles

Page 72

7 phones, 2 dolls, 4 robots

1 train, 10 cars, 2 tea pots

Page 73-76

1. D	2. C	3. C	4. D
5. D	6. D	7. C	8. A
9. B	10. C	11. D	12. A

SCHOLASTIC Learning Express

Congratulations!

I,

_____

am a Scholastic Superstar!

Paste a photo or draw a
picture of yourself.

I have completed Shapes and Patterns K1.

Presented on _____

For page 24

For page 62-64

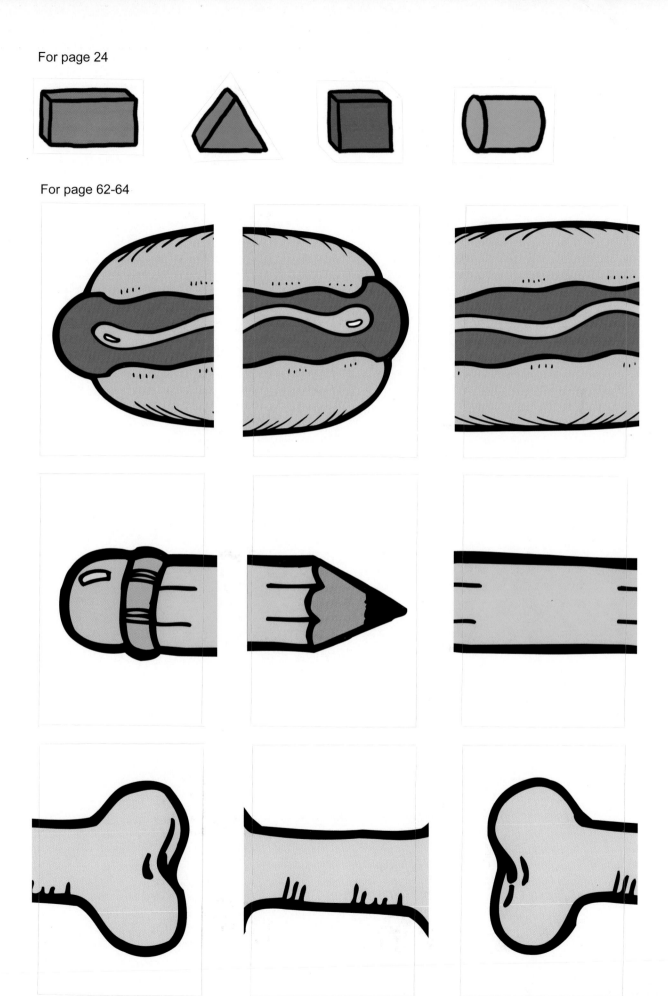

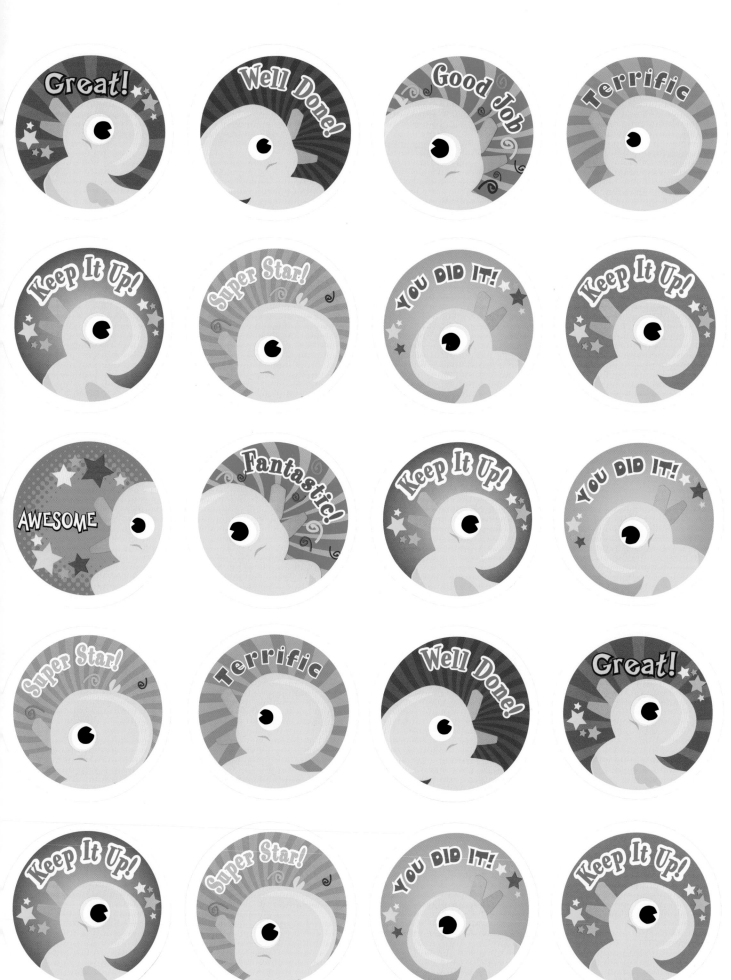